WALKING TO BUCHENWALD

Tom Jacobson

D1519937

BROADWAY PLAY PUBLISHING INC
New York
www.broadwayplaypub.com
info@broadwayplaypub.com

Cover photo by Darrett Sanders

First edition: December 2017
I S B N: 978-0-88145-749-0

Book design: Marie Donovan
Page make-up: Adobe InDesign
Typeface: Palatino

WALKING TO BUCHENWALD was first produced by Open Fist Theatre Company (Martha Demson, Artistic Director & Producer) on 15 September 2017 at Atwater Village Theatre. The cast and creative contributors were:

MILDRED .... Laura James
ROGER .... Ben Martin
SCHILLER .... Christopher Cappiello/Mandy Schneider
ARJAY .... Amielynn Abellera/Justin Huen
others .... Will Bradley

Director .... Roderick Menzies
Set design .... Richard Hoover
Lighting design .... Ellen Monocroussos
Costume design .... Kharen Zeunert
Sound design .... Peter Carlstedt
Production stage manager .... Deena Tovar
Publicity .... Lucy Pollock

CHARACTERS & SETTING

(Five actors)

SCHILLER, *30s-40s, director of strategic planning for a natural history museum*

ARJAY, *30s-40s, a painter and graphic designer*

MILDRED, *70s, retired elementary school teacher, SCHILLER's mother*

ROGER, *70s, retired theatre professor, SCHILLER's father*

Others (played by one actor)

MUSEUM GUIDE *(London)*

HOST *(Bath)*

VISITOR *(Cornwall)*

SERVER *(Paris)*

STUDENT *(Berlin)*

NUDE *(Berlin)*

MINNESOTAN *(Weimar)*

SCHLITZEN *(Weimar)*

BUS DRIVER *(Buchenwald)*

Note: SCHILLER, ARJAY, *and the others may be male or female.*

The play takes in place in various locations in England, France, and Germany.

It is the present.

All locations should be delineated by lighting on a very simple set suggestive of stone. Five chairs and a table might suffice.

ACT ONE

(At rise: MILDRED *isolated in light, seated facing out, with* ROGER *over her shoulder.)*

ROGER: Say no.

MILDRED: No.

*(*SCHILLER *also isolated in light, seated facing out.)*

SCHILLER: I just asked you to think about it.

ROGER: We don't have to think about it.

MILDRED: *(Overlapping)* We don't have to think about it.

ROGER: It's too expensive.

MILDRED: *(Overlapping)* It's too expensive.

SCHILLER: What do you want? A party in the church basement? A quilt with squares by all your friends?

ROGER: All I want is rhubarb pie.

MILDRED: Our friends don't quilt.

ROGER:	SCHILLER:
Put that about the pie.	I'm not paying for a party in the church basement. They're so depressing!
MILDRED:	Don't you want this to
Stop dictating!	be unique? It's once-in-a-lifetime!

MILDRED: You don't have to pay.

ROGER & MILDRED: It's potluck!

SCHILLER: I hate potluck! Somebody always brings a slimy rhubarb pie. Yours should be different.

MILDRED: *Strawberry* rhubarb!

ROGER: Very good.

SCHILLER: Just think about it.

MILDRED: We don't speak any languages.

ROGER:	SCHILLER:
I speak German.	You don't have to! I know a little French, and nobody else cares.

MILDRED: Oh, hardly.

ROGER: We couldn't let you pay.

MILDRED: *(Overlapping)* It's too much for you to pay.

ROGER: We'd have to chip in.

MILDRED: Roger!

SCHILLER: I'll pay your airfare. That's the biggest chunk. Would that work?

ROGER: You'd be with us the whole time?

MILDRED: Roger, I'd never sleep!

ROGER: Type!

MILDRED: Your father wants to know would you be with us the whole time?

ROGER: *(Overlapping)* I've always wanted to see theatre in London.

MILDRED:	SCHILLER:
You have not. You've never said a word.	Of course—I wouldn't unleash you on Europe without adult supervision.

ROGER: You could do genealogy in England and France. Last I heard my mother's cousin still had

family in Germany. Imagine meeting real European
relatives, seeing where we come from—!

MILDRED: Would Arjay go?

SCHILLER: *(Brought up short)* Arjay!

(Lights out instantly on SCHILLER, MILDRED, *and* ROGER,
and up simultaneously on ARJAY *on the telephone isolated
in light)*

ARJAY: Where? When? *Your parents?!*

(Lights up on SCHILLER *on the telephone)*

SCHILLER: You don't have to, but I think they'd come if
they knew you were going.

ARJAY: What about Bolivia?

SCHILLER: Can't that wait till next year? I don't know
enough Spanish yet.

ARJAY: They won't go if it's just you?

SCHILLER: You're a buffer.

ARJAY: Thanks, baby. I'm a buffer. You can't just *send*
them?

SCHILLER: They don't speak any languages.

ARJAY: Send them to England.

SCHILLER: They can't even understand New Yorkers.
This is an important anniversary. Imagine when we've
been together that long.

ARJAY: Gross.

SCHILLER: This is the only time in their entire lives
they'll have the chance to go to Europe. In a year or
two they couldn't manage. I want to do something nice
for them.

ARJAY: Even if they don't want it?

SCHILLER: They never want anything!

ARJAY: Three weeks? They'll drive you crazy whether I'm there or not. There's a reason you don't live in Oklahoma.

SCHILLER: This is a big deal. They'll dine out on it for the rest of their lives. Even if it's miserable.

ARJAY: What if *we're* miserable?

SCHILLER: It'll be a great time to tell them our news.

ARJAY: Can't we just tell them over the phone?

SCHILLER: I don't want it to be that casual. It's a big deal, too, and it might be a bit of a shock to them.

ARJAY: Whatever you want, baby.

SCHILLER: And next year—La Paz!

(Lights out on ARJAY *and up on* MILDRED *and* ROGER. SCHILLER *puts down the phone.)*

MILDRED: We've decided Roger will go with you.

SCHILLER: But this is your anniversary!

ROGER: You wouldn't sleep.

MILDRED: *(Overlapping)* I'd get insomnia.

SCHILLER: Dad, would that be okay coming without Mom?

ROGER: We agreed to it.

MILDRED: *(Overlapping)* Yes.

SCHILLER: You both have to go. It'll change your lives. You'll be different people.

MILDRED: We like who we are.

SCHILLER: Mom, this is just some sort of Midwestern nobody-in-our-family-ever-traveled-so-neither should-we sort of thing. You think you don't deserve to travel, that only rich people travel, but it's not that expensive. I used to think that, too, until I met Arjay. Treat yourself as if you mattered, for once!

MILDRED: We've just been insulted by our own child.

ROGER: No, just you. *I'm* going.

SCHILLER: Are you there? Are you typing a rebuttal or a dissertation?

(Overlapping with SCHILLER *as she tries to change places with* ROGER:)

MILDRED: Then you type.

ROGER: I can't! Mildred!

(Lights out instantly on ROGER *and* MILDRED *as the phone rings and* SCHILLER *picks it up.)*

SCHILLER: Hello?

(Lights up instantly on ROGER *on the phone.)*

ROGER: She wouldn't sleep. She's addicted to sleeping pills as it is, and they still don't work.

SCHILLER: Okay, okay, so if it's just you do you still want to go?

ROGER: I wouldn't mind seeing the Royal Shakespeare Company. They never come to Oklahoma.

SCHILLER: We could see them in London or Stratford— or both! And theatre's cheaper in London than New York—

ROGER: And haven't they restored the Old Globe?

SCHILLER: And the British Museum! The Tate Modern! Plus there's a new Darwin Centre at the Natural History Museum—I think I could get us a private tour—

(Lights suddenly up on MILDRED *on another phone.)*

MILDRED: I hate museums!

SCHILLER: Mother! *(A grim silence)* I thought you weren't going.

MILDRED: If I were. I'm tired of museums.

SCHILLER: *(Hand over the phone, hollering)* Arjay, pick up the phone. My mother's trying to hijack our trip.

MILDRED: Roger, you can't walk too far. Too many museums and you'd be sweating— you'd have to sit down—Schiller, don't walk him all over the place. He's got an atrial fibrillation. He shouldn't even fly, much less go running all over Europe. Hello, Arjay, explain to Schiller why we can't go.

ARJAY: *(Appearing, on the phone)* What?

SCHILLER: Talk Mom into going. She's close.

ARJAY: Europe is wonderful, and everyone should go at least once. When I was teaching in Switzerland I'd take the train somewhere new every weekend—Paris, Munich, Nice—

MILDRED: But you speak the languages.

ARJAY: No, I don't. Not one. Everybody speaks English, or mostly.

SCHILLER: I speak French! A little.

ROGER: I speak German. A little.

MILDRED: What about what's going on politically?

ROGER: President Dickhead.

ARJAY: They've got body searches down to an art, especially in Europe.

ROGER: You might enjoy it, Mildred.

MILDRED: I've got nothing for them to grab.

ARJAY: If you don't go, you'll regret it forever. If you do, even if it's a terrible trip—

SCHILLER: *(Overlapping)* It won't be!

ARJAY: *(Overlapping)* —You'll have stories galore about rude Parisians, mean Germans, and uptight Brits.

MILDRED: Oh, it sounds just awful.

SCHILLER: Mother, you don't have to go.

MILDRED: I'm not!

(Lights out instantly on everyone and up on a breezy MUSEUM GUIDE.*)*

MUSEUM GUIDE: *(British accent)* The Darwin Centre is our way of sharing more of our cultural patrimony with the public—and the world. More than one hundred people a day benefit from behind-the-scenes tours of laboratories and collection storage.

(Lights up sequentially on SCHILLER, ARJAY, ROGER, *and finally, after a pause,* MILDRED, *who looks annoyed to be there.)*

SCHILLER: Only one hundred?

MUSEUM GUIDE: Conservation reasons, really. Zoological specimens are sensitive to light, changes in temperature, even fluctuations in humidity caused by the presence of human beings.

SCHILLER: I know. I'm the V P of Strategic Planning for the Natural History Museum of Los Angeles County—

MUSEUM GUIDE: Brilliant!

ROGER: Not really. I could show you some report cards—

MUSEUM GUIDE: Pardon?

SCHILLER: Dad!

MILDRED: We're Americans.

MUSEUM GUIDE: Yes, well, I assumed—

SCHILLER: We're in the process of planning a new facility as well, and open storage or at least visible storage is one thing we're considering, but doesn't it defeat the purpose if only a hundred people a day can tour? And the salaries of guides—

ARJAY: Not that we'd wish anybody out of a job—

SCHILLER: No, of course not, sorry—

MUSEUM GUIDE: No offense, truly.

SCHILLER: It just doesn't seem efficient. And with the economy the way it is—

MUSEUM GUIDE: Museums are much more heavily subsidized by the government here than in the States. You're at the mercy of the market, aren't you?

SCHILLER: We are, indeed.

ROGER: Scholarship actually has value in England.

MUSEUM GUIDE: Oh, I'm sure in the U S—

ROGER: I'm a college professor—or was until I retired—when was it Mildred—?

MILDRED: A *long* time ago.

ROGER: And I made less—

SCHILLER: Dad, don't—

ROGER: *(Overlapping)* —Than Schiller used to as a secretary—

SCHILLER:	MILDRED:
That was a *really* long time ago—	Mind you, we live in Oklahoma—

ROGER: Forty-fifth, was it, in the nation, for education funding—?

MILDRED: Forty eighth.

SCHILLER: About how many specimens in the zoology collections of the Darwin Centre?

MUSEUM GUIDE: Super question! There are more than sixty million precious specimens in the Life Sciences collections. For instance, these bats—

(SCHILLER, MILDRED, ROGER *and* ARJAY *all lean in to look.*)

MUSEUM GUIDE: —Are just a sample of the *Chiroptera* collections—

ROGER: That's Latin, Mildred. *Amo, amas, amat.*

MUSEUM GUIDE: But if you step this way, we can go directly into storage, where you can see where we keep the rest of the bats—

ROGER: You go on. I'll wait here.

SCHILLER: Dad, this is the behind-the-scenes part. *(To* MUSEUM GUIDE*)* It's not long, is it?

MUSEUM GUIDE: We can breeze right through if you like. Just for a sampling.

ROGER: No, I'm fine to sit.

MILDRED: I think we're jet-lagging, Schiller.

ROGER: Do you want to go back to the hotel, Mildred?

MILDRED: No, I'm all right for now.

ROGER: It's almost time for our nap.

SCHILLER: You'll never get over the jet lag if you sleep now—

ARJAY: Schiller—

ROGER: *(To* MUSEUM GUIDE*)* You have to remember, we're old.

MUSEUM GUIDE: Oh, now—

SCHILLER: I'm sorry. I think we'll have to cut this short.

ROGER: No, no, go on and we'll meet you here.

ARJAY: Don't you need your nap?

MILDRED: We can wait.

ROGER: As long as it's not too long. I'm sorry—I spent too much time with the Belgian Marbles—

MILDRED: Elgin, Roger.

ROGER: Wanted to see them before you have to give 'em back to Greece.

MUSEUM GUIDE: That's unlikely, actually.

SCHILLER: If you take a nap will you be able to go to the theatre later?

MILDRED: Oh, no. Just dinner will be fine.

ROGER: It's too expensive.

SCHILLER: Theatre here is *cheap*!

ROGER: It's enough just to *be* in London. *(To* MUSEUM GUIDE*)* Ever been to America?

MUSEUM GUIDE:	SCHILLER:
Canada, once.	It's too late. I already bought tickets.
ROGER:	MILDRED:
I mean the United States.	Can't you exchange them?
MUSEUM GUIDE:	SCHILLER:
I'm afraid not. But I'd love to see the Grand Canyon.	That's why we're here, so Dad can see London theatre!

MILDRED: Where in Canada did you go?

MUSEUM GUIDE: Toronto. I was visiting relatives on holiday.

MILDRED:	ROGER:
Roger, what's-their-names moved to Toronto. From Sauk Centre.	Who?

ROGER:
Anhorns?

SCHILLER:
I'm going even if you don't.

MILDRED: That's right. Merle and Shirley Anhorn.

MUSEUM GUIDE:
How absolutely bizarre!

SCHILLER:
Arjay, do we know anyone here?

MILDRED:
Do you know them?

ARJAY:
In London? Why?

MUSEUM GUIDE:
They were my uncle's tenants. They took a flat in his building. He's rather spherical, isn't he? And she's got an unusual—

SCHILLER:
We have to do something with these tickets.

MILDRED: Wig.

MUSEUM GUIDE: I was going to say hairstyle.

MILDRED: It's a wig. Hasn't changed in thirty years.

MUSEUM GUIDE: Amazing that you know them!

ROGER: Mildred can connect with anybody. Since you know the Anhorns, you're practically family. If you're ever in Oklahoma, we've got Schiller's old room—

SCHILLER: Dad!

(Lights out on everyone but ROGER.)

ROGER: The perfect theatre audience. We subscribe to the O C U theatre season and then Lyric in the summer—musicals only, but sometimes they're pretty good. For Oklahoma. Theatre audiences are graying all over the country—they all look like us. College educated, some with advanced degrees. Good old-fashioned liberal arts education that's fallen into disrepute as impractical. I heard of a poll—this was in the eighties—they asked students the same question they asked in the sixties and in the seventies: "Why do you go to college?" In the seventies the answer was, overwhelmingly, "To get an education, to learn." By the eighties it was "To get a better job." Remember who was President then. Knowledge for its own sake was suddenly tainted, suspect. You don't want to be too smart because that's, well, un-American. But that's who's going to the theatre— intelligent, educated people who remember what theatre's about. *Liberals,* God forbid!

(Lights up on SCHILLER, ARJAY *and* MILDRED *with* ROGER.)

ARJAY: Mildred, did you like it?

MILDRED: Arjay, I don't know if I've told you this before, but I'm incapable of anticipation. I can't get excited about anything coming up, and I don't know why. Just habit, I suppose, trying prevent disappointment.

SCHILLER: That is so Minnesotan.

ARJAY: So you weren't excited about seeing the play?

MILDRED: No, not at all.

ROGER: She's never excited about seeing a play. Not even when I was directing.

SCHILLER: I'm sorry you didn't like it, Mom. *The Winter's Tale* isn't Shakespeare's best, but I thought this was an excellent production—

MILDRED: Oh, Schiller, it was just wonderful! I didn't know Shakespeare could be *good!*

ROGER: Hey!

MILDRED: I've only seen Shakespeare done by student actors.

ROGER: But they were *my* students!

MILDRED: I know, Roger, but they were students. These were *actors*.

SCHILLER: See! It was like pulling teeth to get you to go—

ROGER: Mildred, my shoe's untied.

MILDRED: *(Kneeling to tie ROGER's shoe)* And I could *understand* them all!

SCHILLER: It helped that it was set in the American south. Mother, what are you doing?

ROGER: She is tying my shoe.

SCHILLER: You can't tie your shoe?

ROGER: I can. But.

MILDRED: He gets out of breath bending over like that. It's just easier if I do it.

SCHILLER: What's your doctor say about that?

ROGER: Lose weight, exercise, same damn thing every doctor says. Are you gonna say it, too?

SCHILLER: Heaven forbid. But still, tying your shoes—

ROGER: Does your bathroom have a washcloth?

ARJAY: How about some dinner?

ROGER & MILDRED: Ours doesn't.

ARJAY: Indian food is great in London.

ROGER: But it's got curry.

ARJAY: The best curry outside of India.

SCHILLER: What's wrong with curry?

ROGER: It's—what's the word, Mildred—?

MILDRED: Cloying.

ROGER:	SCHILLER:
That's right, it's cloying.	Cloying?!

ARJAY: What's cloying?

ROGER:	MILDRED:	SCHILLER:
Sickly sweet.	Overly sweet.	Like it's going bad.

SCHILLER: When have you had curry?

MILDRED: The Burralls made it for us. And they lived in India when Elmer was a missionary.

ROGER: And it was—

EVERYBODY: Cloying!

(Lights out on everyone and simultaneously up on the HOST *of a bed and breakfast.)*

HOST: Now the weir is quite interesting. It's a double weir, very rare, and you can't miss it as you cross the bridge.

(Lights up on MILDRED, ARJAY *and* SCHILLER.)

MILDRED & ARJAY: What's a weir?

SCHILLER: A fish trap, isn't it?

HOST: Or a dam. It's actually quite dangerous.

MILDRED: We don't have those in the States. But Roger loves to fish. Schiller, too.

ARJAY: You're kidding.

SCHILLER: Not since I was a kid.

MILDRED: One time when Schiller was three, they were catching sunfish after sunfish, none of the usual waiting around slapping mosquitoes. Fish just kept coming without a break. Finally Schiller threw down the pole and announced, "Me all done fittin'!"

SCHILLER: Ma!

MILDRED: Schiller is easily embarrassed. You should just accept that we're your parents and we're going to be embarrassing.

SCHILLER: I'm not embarrassed, but not everybody wants to hear about—

HOST: Oh, no! I love hearing about peoples' lives, especially Americans. That's why we started a bed and breakfast. Where are you from?

MILDRED: Roger taught theatre at Oklahoma City University, and I taught gradeschool until I couldn't stand it any more—discipline was all it was—and then I managed a shop in a science museum.

HOST: Were you there for the bombing?

SCHILLER: They felt it!

MILDRED: It shook the house. We live near the railroad, so we thought a tanker had exploded.

HOST: Did you…know anyone…?

MILDRED: No.

SCHILLER: A girl I went to school with. But I didn't really know her.

MILDRED: I don't believe in capital punishment, but—

SCHILLER: Oh, our whole justice system sucks. Three strikes—overcrowded prisons—

MILDRED: Don't get me started!

ARJAY: The memorial is beautiful.

SCHILLER: Only decent design in the entire state.

MILDRED: It's a very conservative state. We're the only Democrats we know.

SCHILLER: We don't live there. Arjay teaches at Art Center College of Design in Pasadena—

HOST: How interesting! I really do love Americans. Only been to New York and Washington, and Florida. Never to Los Angeles or Oklahoma—

SCHILLER: Not much to see.

MILDRED: Roger and I are from Minnesota, but we couldn't take the cold. And Oklahomans are nice, even if they all belong to the John Birch Society.

HOST: All Americans are nice. Except New Yorkers. We had this Jewish couple stay here and they complained about everything—

SCHILLER: New Yorkers always complain—it doesn't matter who—

HOST: The bed was too soft, the toast was cold. I moved them to the haunted room.

ARJAY: There's a haunted room?

SCHILLER: That is so cool! How does it—manifest?

HOST: Sometimes there's a woman who sits on the bed.

MILDRED:	ARJAY:	SCHILLER:
Ish, I got a chill!	Have you seen her?	What period are her clothes?

HOST: My daughter saw her. I think she's from the eighteenth century. That's when most of Bath was built, but this house is a little bit older. She seems friendly.

ARJAY: So what else should we see other than the weird?

SCHILLER: Weir.

ARJAY: Other than the dam fish trap.

SCHILLER: We need to see the Abbey Church, the Royal Crescent, and of course the Roman baths.

ARJAY: Can we go in?

HOST: Oh, no! Absolutely teeming with bacteria. Once you see it you won't *want* to go in!

SCHILLER: Don't worry. I've got it all planned out to minimize walking.

ARJAY: Schiller plans.

SCHILLER: Somebody has to! Arjay's been all over the world without a plan.

ARJAY: I never had a problem.

SCHILLER: That's because the universe takes care of you. It's amazing—you don't speak anything, and yet people always help you—

ARJAY: Schiller planned this whole trip, in case you can't guess.

SCHILLER:	MILDRED:
I'm part of the universe that takes care of you.	And you've done a wonderful job—I can hardly believe it!

ARJAY: What's that Italian saying?

SCHILLER: *L'uomo propone, e Dio dispone.*

MILDRED: What's that mean?

ARJAY: Man plans—

SCHILLER: Man proposes, God disposes. But people like you need people like me. I'm the kind of person who gets things done.

ARJAY: You're the kind of person who makes the trains run on time.

MILDRED: Oh, the trains here are amazing! We only have Amtrak at home and it always seems to be falling apart.

HOST: Isn't the whole country falling apart?

MILDRED: What?

SCHILLER: What do you mean?

HOST: Not to be rude, but your president is a real D H.

ARJAY: D H?

HOST: A real dickhead!

MILDRED: That's what Roger calls him! Roger!

ROGER: *(Off)* Just a minute, Mildred! I'm eating!

HOST: He's got no notion whatsoever of foreign policy.

ROGER. *(Comes in, wiping his mouth)* What am I missing in here?

MILDRED: We're talking politics. *American* politics! *(To HOST)* I hardly watch any television, but I never miss *Washington Week in Review.* I don't care about movies, music, sports—and Roger can hardly drag me to a play, but I love politics! You don't know how isolated we feel in Oklahoma. They all think the president is wonderful.

ROGER: President Dickhead.

MILDRED: See!

HOST: D H was my attempt at politesse.

ROGER: He's crazy. A real D H!

SCHILLER: How was breakfast?

ROGER: Just wonderful! I ate your bacon for you.

SCHILLER: *(To HOST)* It was very good, but if we're not careful these English breakfasts can really add up.

ROGER: Are you implying—?

SCHILLER: Nothing, Dad, nothing! I just don't want to eat too much. We've got a lot of ground to cover today.

MILDRED: Not too much ground. We hardly ever walk at home.

HOST: Bath is quite compact. You can see most of it on foot.

SCHILLER: So I won't have to drive at all!

ROGER: And a good thing, too! When we first rented the car—

SCHILLER: Gimme a break! It's the first time I ever drove on the left!

ROGER: —Schiller drove too close to the curb and all of a sudden the sideview mirror was in Arjay's lap!

MILDRED:	SCHILLER:
We never did see what we hit.	They don't give you any instructions at the rental place. No rules of the road, no tips about driving on the left.
ARJAY:	
I just popped the mirror back on.	

ROGER: You almost killed us on that first roundabout!

SCHILLER: Dad!

HOST: *How* many days is your trip?

(Lights out on everyone but SCHILLER *and* ARJAY, *who are isolated in light together.)*

ARJAY: They're not so bad.

SCHILLER: They're not *your* parents.

ARJAY: They hardly complain at all, and they're so grateful. It could have been so much worse.

SCHILLER: They're too goddam friendly! The British are reserved!

ARJAY: You're too easily embarrassed.

SCHILLER: It's hard enough being an American in Europe right now, but they make me feel like a resentful teenager again—like magic!

ARJAY: If I haven't said so before, I think it's really nice you're doing this for them.

SCHILLER: I'm a good kid?

ARJAY: You're a good kid. *(Kissing* SCHILLER.)

SCHILLER: You realize that's the first time we've kissed this whole trip?

ARJAY: *(Shrugs)* That's what happens around parents. I'm sure you'll be very happy you did this—

ARJAY & SCHILLER: —When it's over. *(They sit down in two chairs next to each other.)*

SCHILLER: This is definitely the most exciting thing they've ever done in their lives. They're not exactly accomplished.

ARJAY: But it *is* amazing how much breakfast your father can put away. That's an accomplishment!

SCHILLER: And he starts asking about lunch by ten a.m.!

(Lights up on MILDRED *and* ROGER *seated directly behind* SCHILLER *and* ARJAY. SCHILLER *is driving.)*

ROGER: I think your mother's getting a little hungry.

SCHILLER: We just ate.

ROGER: She's borderline hypoglycemic.

MILDRED: Hush, Roger. I'm not hungry. But if there's a turn-off soon, I need to go to the bathroom.

ROGER: *(To* ARJAY*)* Mildred is always hungry, thirsty, or has to go to the bathroom.

SCHILLER: Whereas Dad is always hungry.

ROGER: Enough to eat curry.

ARJAY: And you liked it!

ROGER: It was surprisingly good. Not—

EVERYONE: —Cloying!

SCHILLER: That's what's good about travel—you end up trying things you never thought you'd like.

MILDRED: How far away are we from the Crossett site?

ARJAY: Is that a stone circle?

SCHILLER: It's a genealogical site. The Crossetts were—

MILDRED: My father's mother's family. Sherm and Caryl saw some Crossett graves in Cornwall. Near here, is that right, Schiller?

SCHILLER: Kinda.

ARJAY: Are you having a good time, Mildred?

MILDRED: Oh, yes, Arjay, it's just wonderful.

ARJAY: Aren't you glad I talked you into coming? *(Pause)* You weren't going to until I talked to you.

ROGER: *(Starting to tear up)* That's not exactly—

MILDRED: Roger, hush.

ROGER: She has a real reason.

SCHILLER:	ARJAY:
What?	Roger, what's wrong?

MILDRED:	ROGER:
(Quickly)	Nothing. A bug flew in my
Thank you, Arjay.	eye. Close the window.

MILDRED: Thanks for talking me into it.

ROGER: It'd be no fun without Mildred.

MILDRED: I just had to find my reason.

ARJAY: Genealogy? Finding out who you are?

MILDRED: That's part of it.

ARJAY: What else?

SCHILLER: We don't have time to go to—!

MILDRED: Look out, here's another circle-round!

SCHILLER: Roundabout, Mother, roundabout!

MILDRED: Careful—I have to pee!

(They all lean the same direction for a fast turn. Lights out on them and up on VISITOR drinking from a paper cup. In the dark, the chairs are rearranged. VISITOR sits. Lights up

on SCHILLER, ARJAY, MILDRED *and* ROGER, *seated, eating some form of prepackaged convenience food.* ROGER *eats enthusiastically.)*

SCHILLER: The Eden Project is a perfect model for museums of the future. Its message is everywhere—sustainability *is* possible. See? The seating is recycled tires, everything we're eating is grown locally and organically.

ROGER: Right here in Devon?

SCHILLER: Cornwall, Dad. We passed through Devon on the way here.

ROGER: A long scary drive on the left side.

SCHILLER: American museums are too old-fashioned, passive. These displays are thoughtful, integrated, with action items outlined—Americans have the largest ecological footprint of any people in the world, but if we—

(MILDRED *sees the* VISITOR *and pauses in her eating.* SCHILLER *sees where she is looking.)*

SCHILLER: Mother, no.

MILDRED: Eating alone is so awful.

SCHILLER: No. Please.

MILDRED: It's a wasted day unless you talk to the local people. I don't know what I'll do in France and Germany since I don't speak the language.

SCHILLER: These are very reserved people—

MILDRED: Would you like to join us?

(VISITOR *reacts with surprise.)*

Would you? I hate eating alone, don't you?

VISITOR: *(Joining them)* I don't want to intrude.

MILDRED: Not at all. Please sit down. I'm Mildred and this is my husband, Roger.

VISITOR:	ROGER:
Hello.	Hi there.

SCHILLER: I'm Schiller.

MILDRED: And this is Schiller's friend, Arjay.

ARJAY: How do you do?

VISITOR: I'm Beverly.

ROGER & MILDRED: We're Americans.

SCHILLER: As if you couldn't guess.

VISITOR: You can always tell Americans on holiday. They look like giant six year-olds in short trousers.

MILDRED: Beverly's such a British name. Do people call you Bev?

VISITOR: No, Beverly. Don't get so many Americans as we used to.

MILDRED: This is our first time to England.

ROGER: To Europe!

ARJAY & SCHILLER: We've been before.

ROGER: Bet you've seen a real drop-off in tourism since—

VISITOR: It's about to get worse.

MILDRED: What do you mean?

ROGER: Did something happen? Our dickhead president—

VISITOR: Your hotel room doesn't have telly?

SCHILLER: It's a bed and breakfast, and both T Vs only showed cartoons. Plus my phone coverage is spotty here.

ARJAY: Your batteries are for shit.

ROGER: And no washcloth! Again! Must be some kind of regulation.

MILDRED: What happened?

VISITOR: Your president—

MILDRED & ROGER: Not *our!*

ROGER, ARJAY & SCHILLER: We didn't vote for him!

VISITOR: Well, he's your president, just the same, isn't he?

MILDRED: What are we supposed to do, assassinate him?

SCHILLER:	ROGER:
Mother!	Mildred!

MILDRED: Well, we voted. What good did it do? What's an average person supposed to do?

ROGER: I think we have to trust the system. It's the best system of government in the world. I came of age between wars, so I never fought for it, but I would have, maybe not for Vietnam, but—

VISITOR: But it's breaking down, isn't it?

ROGER: At least we were never an empire like England or France—

SCHILLER:	VISITOR:
Dad, calm down.	All republics degenerate into empires eventually.

ARJAY: What do you mean breaking down?

VISITOR: Your election process—

ROGER:	ARJAY:
Just wait till the next one.	The pendulum will swing.

VISITOR: And now, with this tactical alert—

MILDRED:	SCHILLER:	ARJAY:
Tactical alert?	What's that mean?	Why?

VISITOR: On account of the plot to blow up the airport in Los Angeles.

SCHILLER:	ARJAY:
What?	L A X?

VISITOR: They caught them, or so they said.

SCHILLER: That's at least the third time—

MILDRED:	ARJAY:
But what does tactical alert mean?	Should we go home?

SCHILLER: Home? And fly right into the target?

VISITOR: Ambassadors recalled. Again. Americans evacuated—

ROGER: Don't worry—checks and balances—

VISITOR: Pretty unchecked at this point.

MILDRED: I wonder if there really was a plot. It might just be an excuse.

ROGER: Like I said, we're hardly dashing to become the next evil empire.

VISITOR: That usually happens slowly—more like a walk. But it's getting brisker, isn't it?

ROGER: We're not Germany!

VISITOR: Germany took a long time to become Germany. Hitler was just exploiting the German character.

ROGER: The German character? You're still not over the War, are you? You're prejudiced against Germans. I'm part German.

MILDRED: In fact, if you counted the English, Welsh, Irish, and Scottish as separate groups, Germans are the largest ancestral group in America.

VISITOR: I'm not suggesting panic. But we've seen a lot of this before, haven't we?

ROGER: *(Sighs, defeated)* Mildred's right—what can one person do?

MILDRED: Remember that old moral question that we used to fantasize about? If you could go back in time and assassinate Hitler would you?

ROGER:	SCHILLER:	ARJAY:
Of course!	You used to fantasize about that?	In a minute.

VISITOR: Right.

MILDRED: What if in the future people are saying that about our president—and we were the ones who had the opportunity to kill him, but didn't?

ROGER: Mildred, don't talk like that!

SCHILLER: I think they can arrest you for even saying that, Mother.

VISITOR: But you're not in America, are you?

MILDRED: Exactly! Roger, imagine that! I actually feel freer here than in America. *(Loudly)* Assassinate the president!

SCHILLER:	ROGER:	ARJAY:
Mother, hush!	Mildred!	Jesus!

MILDRED: Oh, I'll be quiet. But think about it.

SCHILLER: When we get home you can go to a demonstration.

MILDRED: I'm too old to go marching. My hips would protest louder than I can.

ARJAY: Rosa Parks changed everything by just sitting down.

MILDRED: I have to carry a board with me to sit on— *(Shows it)*

SCHILLER: Oh, Mom, don't—

ROGER: We call it her butt board.

MILDRED: I got osteoporosis which led to sciatica, so after I had a bone spur removed they gave me estrogen, but of course in those days they didn't know how much to give so apparently I overdosed because in a few years I had to have a mastectomy—

SCHILLER: Mom, I'm sure—

MILDRED: And then five years later, I lost the *other* breast—

SCHILLER: *(To* VISITOR*)* You don't want to hear this, do you—?

VISITOR: It's all right.

MILDRED: And then five years after that— *(Digs in her purse)* —I had to have a hysterectomy—

SCHILLER: Mom, no—!

MILDRED: *(Pulling a Polaroid from her purse)* You want to see a picture of my cyst?

SCHILLER: Mom, put that away.

VISITOR: *(Looking at the Polaroid)* It looks like a deflated beach ball.

ROGER: As big as a cantaloupe.

SCHILLER: A grapefruit.

MILDRED & ROGER: A cantaloupe!

ARJAY: *(To* SCHILLER*)* Thank God they don't speak French.

(Lights out on everyone except SCHILLER*)*

SCHILLER: The whole concept of museums started in the eighteenth century with cabinets of curiosities, usually brought back from voyages overseas. Natural specimens, cultural objects, all displayed as if—"isn't this weird? Aren't you glad we're not like that?" The British pioneered this kind of display, exploiting public fascination with oddities and deformities. This museum was founded by a taxidermist. Can you tell?

(Lights up on ARJAY, MILDRED *and* ROGER *with* SCHILLER, *peering at a display.)*

ROGER: A goat with seven legs.

MILDRED: Poor little thing. It didn't live very long, did it?

ROGER: Growing up on the farm, I saw one or two stillborn calves with extra legs.

ARJAY: Oh, wow, look at this.

(They move on to another display.)

ROGER: Guinea pigs playing cricket.

MILDRED: It's cute, but creepy.

ARJAY: *(Looking at another display)* Oh, no. This is worse.

SCHILLER: Kittens serving tea.

ARJAY: Oh, my God, look.

ROGER: *(Reading a label)* "These kittens were not killed for this display."

MILDRED:	SCHILLER:
Oh, ish.	Right.

ARJAY: Never mind that they're all the exact same kind of kittens at exactly the same age.

SCHILLER: I bet farmers knew he liked kittens and brought bags of them freshly drowned.

ROGER: That's what you do in the country. If animals are no use, you get rid of 'em.

MILDRED: Schiller, we've been to a lot of museums on this trip—

ARJAY: This one barely qualifies—

MILDRED: Aren't we close to the Crossett site, that church—?

SCHILLER: It's kinda out of the way, Mom.

ARJAY: I'm sick of museums, too. When are we going to see stone circles?

SCHILLER: The Hurlers are out on Bodmin Moor, just a few miles south. I figured we could see them after lunch.

ROGER: Your mother and I have to have our nap after lunch.

SCHILLER: Then Arjay and I will have to see the Hurlers without you. Trethevy Quoit is there, too.

ARJAY: What's that?

SCHILLER: They're not sure. Might be part of a prehistoric barrow tomb. Or maybe a mini Stonehenge.

MILDRED: So the Crossett site is too far away?

SCHILLER: I think so, Mom. We're only here for a day and you have to have your nap.

MILDRED: I need an acetaminophen before I can sleep.

ROGER: What are the Hurlers?

ARJAY: A stone circle.

SCHILLER: Three of them actually.

MILDRED: Oh, I wanted to see those.

SCHILLER: Do you want to nap in the car on the way?

MILDRED: No, I have to lie down. Don't worry about the Crossett site. Caryl and Sherm have pictures, I'm sure.

SCHILLER: And we don't know exactly where it is. We'd spend the whole afternoon on a wild goose chase. Our time is limited.

ROGER: How soon is lunch?

SCHILLER:	ARJAY:
Soon, Dad!	Now, if you're hungry.

SCHILLER: He's always hungry.

ROGER: Yes, and then I will be sleepy. That's what it's like to be seventy-damn-something years old!

MILDRED: Roger, your blood sugar is low.

SCHILLER: We'll eat right away. There's a pub next door.

ROGER: And then I want a nap.

MILDRED: Oh, I looked in that pub. I'd rather not.

ARJAY: Are you tired of pub food?

MILDRED: I don't mind pubs, but this one smelled worse than usual.

ROGER: Well, we have to eat.

ARJAY: Soon.

SCHILLER: Okay, okay! We'll eat as soon as we can find the exact right kind of restaurant that doesn't smell, even if it means driving through one-way lanes for miles! And then we'll come all the way back here so you can have your nap	MILDRED: All right, we can eat at the pub. ARJAY: Could we get room service?

and then we'll drive some more so we can see the fucking stone circles and I'm sorry but we're not going to wander all over Cornwall looking for dead relatives!	ROGER: That's too expensive! And I bet the hotel doesn't even have room service.

ROGER: Last night I dreamed about a washcloth. Don't they have them in England at all?

(Lights out. French music begins, possibly La Marseillaise. The lights come back up with a beautiful stained-glass window effect.)

(MILDRED, ROGER and ARJAY stand transfixed. After a moment, MILDRED reads from a brochure.)

MILDRED: Saint Chapelle was the private chapel of Louis—what is that?—the ninth, I think—and was built to house the relics of the crown of thorns and a piece of the True Cross. Louis the ninth—later Saint Louis— paid more for the relics than he did for the entire chapel.

ROGER: This is the most beautiful church I've ever been in. Just look at those windows!

ARJAY: And the afternoon sun is hitting them just right.

SCHILLER: *(Appearing with phone)* I planned it that way. I really wanted you to see this.

MILDRED:	ROGER:
Schiller, it's wonderful!	Just magnificent!

ROGER: Is there a book? I want to buy a book.

SCHILLER: *(Taking a picture)* Hold still—I'll take your picture.

ROGER: I still want a book.

SCHILLER: Okay, we'll get a book. There's a shop downstairs. Shall we go?

ARJAY: We just got here!

ROGER: I want to sit and look.

MILDRED: I really need to sit, Roger.

SCHILLER: But not too long if we're going to make it to the Pompidou before it closes.

ARJAY: Schiller, we just got to Paris.

MILDRED: ARJAY:
We've already seen Notre   Your poor parents...!
Dame, the Seine—

ROGER: Had lunch! It was very good.

MILDRED: But we haven't had our nap.

SCHILLER: You napped in the Chunnel!

ARJAY: Shhh! This *is* a chapel...

ROGER: I slept right through it!

MILDRED: I didn't sleep.

ARJAY: Don't be a travel Nazi.

SCHILLER: All right, we can skip the Pompidou.

ROGER: Your mother's exhausted and her hips hurt. Come sit with me, Mildred, and be my honey.

MILDRED: Don't blame it all on me, Roger. You're the one with the atrial fibrillation.

(ROGER *and* MILDRED *sit, apart from* ARJAY *and* SCHILLER. *Gradually, the lights go out on* ROGER *and* MILDRED.)

ARJAY: They're really doing very well. Overall.

SCHILLER: Surprisingly well. I know. There's just so much I want them to see. It's not like you and I are seeing anything new. This trip is for them.

ARJAY: Which is why we should see it at their pace.

SCHILLER: Walking that slowly feels like I'm stuck in tar.

ARJAY: You've done a great job of planning the whole trip. I haven't had to do a thing.

SCHILLER: And you got to see your stupid stone circles. Took a million photographs.

ARJAY: Thank you, baby. They fit perfectly into my *Ozymandias* series.

SCHILLER: Do you think we should tell them tonight?

ARJAY: I don't know why you're avoiding it.

SCHILLER:	ARJAY:
I'm not avoiding—	You keep putting it off.

SCHILLER: I just want it to be the right moment. I don't know how they'll react.

ARJAY: Tonight's that restaurant in Montmartre, with the Japanese owner—?

SCHILLER: He's not Japanese, he's a Japanophile. He dates a Japanese woman and has a Japanese chef—

ARJAY: —Who makes the best *foie gras*—

SCHILLER: You're right—they're bound to be in a good mood—they'll be eating the best meal of their lives.

ARJAY: Do they know what *foie gras* is?

ROGER: *(In the dark)* What *is* this?

(Lights up on ROGER *and* MILDRED *seated at a table.* SCHILLER *and* ARJAY *join them.)*

SCHILLER, ARJAY & MILDRED: It's *foie gras*!

ROGER: It looks like a baby liver.

ARJAY: It's goose liver.

SCHILLER: They force-feed the goose to make the liver especially rich—

MILDRED: What do they do with the rest of the goose?

ARJAY: Somebody eats it, I'm sure.

MILDRED: I'd just hate to think the poor goose goes through all that—could you imagine—your whole life and you turn out to be nothing but an appetizer!

ROGER: Little goose, little goose, give me your liver! *(In a goose voice)* Oh, no, I'm not! Not even a sliver!

SCHILLER: Dad!

ROGER: Too late little goose! *(Pops the entire foie gras in his mouth)*

ARJAY: Oh, no!

SCHILLER:	MILDRED:
Dad, gross!	Roger!

ROGER: *(His mouth full)* What? You want me to spit it out?

ARJAY: That is so wrong.

SCHILLER: It's an exquisite delicacy. You're supposed to savor it—on toast points!

ROGER: It *was* good. Gone now, though.

ARJAY: At least Mildred can enjoy it slowly.

MILDRED: I don't think I can enjoy it at all. It makes me too sad.

WAITER: *(Appearing)* Did Monsieur enjoy the *foie gras*?

ROGER: Excellent!

WAITER: Would you like another?

ROGER: No, thank you. Apparently my wife doesn't want hers. Mildred?

MILDRED: Go ahead, Roger.

SCHILLER: Ma, you *have* to eat it! It's the best dish in the whole world!

WAITER: *Merci beaucoup.*

SCHILLER:	ROGER:
C'est vrai. But I haven't tried it yet.	Too late! *(Pops the whole foie gras in his mouth.)*

(SCHILLER glares at ROGER.)

ARJAY: This our third time to Paris together and our third time here.

WAITER: *Tres bien.*

SCHILLER: We met the owner last time. What is his name—Marcel?

WAITER: No, no, that is the old owner. How you say—previous?

SCHILLER: He sold the restaurant?

WAITER: *Oui.* Two years almost.

SCHILLER: No!

ARJAY: And the Japanese chef?

WAITER: *(Shrugs)* How can Japanese cook French?

ARJAY: He was very good.

SCHILLER: You fired him?

WAITER: I am not owner.

ARJAY: You have a French chef now?

WAITER: *Oui. Non.* Algerian.

SCHILLER: Algerian!?

WAITER: *Escusez-moi. (Disappears)*

ARJAY: Schiller— *(Looking around)* I think *everyone* here is Algerian.

ROGER: And you said that really loud.

SCHILLER: You're the loud ones!

MILDRED: Are they all looking, or am I paranoid?

ROGER: Algerians are Arabs, aren't they?

SCHILLER: Algeria is in Africa.

ARJAY: But Islamic I think is what your father means.

MILDRED. *(Brightly)* So tomorrow will we go to the Giradelle graveyard? An actual headstone!

SCHILLER: *(Overlapping)* Only if you want to give up three other things. It's outside Paris, so it'll take most of the day—

ARJAY: What's scheduled?

SCHILLER: And you'd miss your nap.

ARJAY: Is tomorrow the Muse De Orsay?

SCHILLER: It's the Musee d'Orsay, but yes. I planned on lunch there—they've got a great buffet—then—God smiles on his pious children—the Louvre is open late.

MILDRED: So I won't be doing *any* genealogy on this trip?

SCHILLER: Ancestors aren't us, Ma. They don't have anything to do with us.

MILDRED:	ROGER:
I think they do in a way.	We can do genealogy in Germany.

MILDRED: That's your side of the family, Roger. What about mine?

SCHILLER: You can't expect the dead to tell you who you are.

MILDRED: You're right. It's fine. It's not like I'm the DAR. It really isn't important in the grand scheme.

SCHILLER: *(After a pause)* Ma, I'm sorry. It's just—we don't have time—

MILDRED: In a hundred years we'll all be dead and none of this will matter.

ARJAY: *(To* SCHILLER*)* You better do a better apology than that.

SCHILLER: Okay, Ma, I know it's important to you, so maybe we can skip the Louvre—

ROGER: Skip the Louvre!?

SCHILLER:	ARJAY:
Dad!	Shhhh!

*(*WAITER *arrives, silently drops off the check, and starts to leave.)*

SCHILLER: Wait a minute, what's this?

WAITER: *(Icy) Pardonnez-moi?*

SCHILLER: What's this? It looks like the check.

WAITER: *Quoi? Qu'est-ce que c'est* "check?"

SCHILLER: *L'addition.*

WAITER: *Oui.*

SCHILLER: We've only had the appetizer. We're here for dinner.

WAITER: *Je ne comprends.*

SCHILLER:	ARJAY:
We ordered entrees.	The *foie gras* was great.

WAITER: *Je ne parle Anglais.*

SCHILLER: You spoke it just fine a minute ago. Okay, *je parle un petit Français*—

*(*WAITER *laughs and leaves.)*

ROGER: *(After a moment)* I don't think we're gonna get served.

SCHILLER: Yes, we are. I'll just have to use my French, which I don't really have.

ARJAY: I suspect we'll be actively ignored until we leave.

SCHILLER: Then we won't leave. We'll just wait until we're waited on.

MILDRED: Oh, no, Schiller, let's not do that.

ROGER: If we're not being treated well, we can go somewhere else.

SCHILLER: This is a special place and it's a special evening and we're going to stay here till it gets special again.

ARJAY: It's not *that* special.

SCHILLER: That's true. The foie gras— *(Louder)* — Wasn't nearly as good as it used to be!

ARJAY:	ROGER:	MILDRED:
Jesus, Schiller!	Shhhhhh!	Sweetie, relax!

ARJAY: You're being a very ugly American at the moment. Stop it!

ROGER: If we have this much trouble with the French, imagine the Germans!

SCHILLER: Fine. I'll be quiet. But we're going to wait.

MILDRED: *(After a few tense moments)* How long?

SCHILLER: *(After a few more tense moments)* Arjay and I have some news we've been saving—

ARJAY: Oh, Schiller, not now!

SCHILLER: No, this is the perfect time. This is when we planned to tell them. And we have— *(Looking around)* —Nothing else to do just now—

ARJAY: You'll taint the moment.

SCHILLER: The moment's *been* tainted.

(ARJAY *gestures "go ahead then."*)

SCHILLER: Arjay and I are getting married.

ROGER: *(After a moment)* In a church?

SCHILLER: In *my* church. The minister's retiring and we want him to perform the ceremony before he goes.

MILDRED: But isn't Arjay kind of an atheist?

ARJAY: I worship all 128 Egyptian gods.

SCHILLER: You always say that, but you take communion at Christmas and Easter.

ARJAY: And the wine boils and the host flies across the room.

SCHILLER: But.

ARJAY: But it's important to Schiller to do it in a Lutheran church.

SCHILLER: So—some good news. *(After a moment of silence)* What do you think?

MILDRED: Schiller, are you sure? Why ruin what you've got?

ROGER:	SCHILLER:
You've been together	Ruin?
eight years—	

SCHILLER: You're trying to talk us out of it?

MILDRED: No, no, of course not. I've just seen so many couples—cohabitate—then when they get married, they break up within a few months.

ARJAY: We're together together. No quickie divorce after a couple of months.

ROGER: *(Toasting)* Well, congratulations. *(Nudging* MILDRED*)* To the happy couple!

(As they clink glasses:)

ARJAY: I've been dying to tell you for weeks.

MILDRED: When?

ARJAY: We've known for, well, months, actually—

MILDRED: No, no. When is the actual ceremony? What date?

SCHILLER: Not for another nine to ten months.

MILDRED: That won't work.

SCHILLER: We have to have time to plan.

MILDRED: No, that's too long.

ARJAY: What do you mean?

MILDRED: Assuming you want me to come.

SCHILLER: Ma, what do you mean? Of course you're invited.

MILDRED: What was that Italian saying? About God and plans?

SCHILLER: *L'uomo propone, e Dio dispone.*

MILDRED: God is disposing—of me.

SCHILLER: *(After a moment)* What...do you mean?

ROGER: Your mother has cancer again, Schiller.

SCHILLER: What...kind?

MILDRED: Colon. Just like Ma and Pa had.

SCHILLER: But treatments have improved since then. They'd still be with us today— Chances are—

MILDRED: It's an operation and then chemo. I'm not going through that again.

SCHILLER: You're...not...

MILDRED: No.

SCHILLER: You'd rather...

MILDRED: Yes.

(SCHILLER stares at MILDRED a moment, forces back tears, then hugs MILDRED very tightly.)

MILDRED: *(While comforting* SCHILLER*)* So your wedding sounds wonderful. Roger and I would love to come. Just sooner than later please, sooner than later.

END OF ACT ONE

ACT TWO

(ARJAY *isolated in light*.)

ARJAY: Three years ago, we saw a lot more Americans at the Hiroshima memorial than at Nagasaki. Which is probably a good thing, because the Nagasaki museum is very—I dunno—forthright about the bombing. Maybe it's because Hiroshima got all the postwar aid, but in Nagasaki they make it quite clear that Japan was ready to surrender before the U.S. dropped either bomb, and that there was an *absolute* lack of necessity to bomb Nagasaki. The only reason they didn't hit a purely military target—like a ship at sea—was to terrify the Soviets and let the world know America not only had the bomb, but was willing to use it on civilians. We're still the only country to actually make a nuclear strike—and we've done it *twice*. The exhibits were very moving, frightening, and exceptionally well designed.

(*Lights up on* SCHILLER, MILDRED *and* ROGER *riding the subway*.)

ROGER: I couldn't do it.

SCHILLER: The Hiroshima museum was too graphic—wax dummies of people with their arms melting off.

ROGER: No, see, I couldn't. Memorials, museums—I know it's important to pay respects, to remember, but sometimes it just seems like a form of entertainment, indulging in emotions, even painful ones—and vaguely, well, immoral.

SCHILLER: Museums are immoral? Catharsis is self-indulgent?

MILDRED: It's learning, isn't it? Knowledge isn't immoral.

ROGER: The Greeks never showed violence in their plays—they'd reveal the bodies afterward and let you imagine how they died. But the characters on stage were clearly responsible, culpable in those deaths. It doesn't work if it's too literal. I heard about a production of *Medea* where they made lifelike dummies of the children that concealed breakable containers of red liquid. When Medea had her revenge on Jason, she just picked up the kids and slammed them face-first into a wall. The audience rioted and the production had to stop.

ARJAY: Are you gonna be all right in the German—how do you say it?

SCHILLER: *Deutsche Historische Museum.*

ARJAY: We can skip the Holocaust part.

MILDRED: No, no. We have to see it. That's why we're here, isn't it?

ROGER: I think we're kind of obligated. To be there at least. I spose I can look away if it's too disturbing. I've seen death camp liberation film footage, but it's not the same as actually being here in Berlin. I keep expecting a swastika around every corner.

ARJAY: Talk about effective design—the swastika's the world's most recognizable political logo. And the Nazis totally *owned* the colors red and black.

MILDRED: *(Looking around)* They look so sad.

SCHILLER: Who?

MILDRED: All the people on this train. Like they're about to cry.

SCHILLER: Maybe you would, too, if you had World War Two on your conscience.

ROGER: I am a doughnut.

SCHILLER: Dad, we just had breakfast.

ROGER: I don't want a doughnut. I am a doughnut.

SCHILLER: *(After a moment)* Why are you a doughnut, Dad?

ROGER: I'm quoting J F K. When he came here and said, *"Ich bin ein Berliner,"* he was actually saying "I'm a jelly doughnut."

ARJAY: You're kidding.

ROGER: He meant to say, *"Ich bin Berliner"* —I am a Berliner. But the article *"ein"* made it into the local name for a raspberry filled doughnut.

MILDRED: He did very well for a pastry.

ROGER: I always wonder what the rest of his presidency would have been like, if he'd gotten a chance—

SCHILLER: Mom, you weren't hanging around a grassy knoll in Dallas in 1963, were you?

MILDRED: I'm never going to live that down, am I?

ROGER & SCHILLER: No.

MILDRED: Do you remember that story told by one of the Nazi guards in the Nuremberg trials about the woman slipping and falling on her way into the gas chamber?

SCHILLER & ARJAY: No.

ROGER: I never heard of that story.

MILDRED: The guard was trying to explain what it felt like to be a part of that horrible machine, how numbed he felt, like he wasn't actually there, only watching, and then he saw that woman fall. Naked, completely vulnerable, no dignity remaining, and she tripped and fell, right at the door to the shower. His instinct was to help her up, but that wasn't his job, and he realized he'd be helping her to her death. In that instant of his hesitation, another woman, just as naked, reached down and helped the fallen woman to her feet. She knew both women were going to die, and that her gift of a moment's dignity to the other woman was noble only for its, well, futility. But she wanted her last act to be a kindness.

ARJAY: He could see all that in her eyes?

MILDRED: He saw it in his heart. At least I like to think he did.

SCHILLER: I think there's a model of Auschwitz in the Deutsche Historische Museum.

(Slowly lights isolate SCHILLER, *who stands.)*

SCHILLER: I hope it's not too crowded there. In Nagasaki there weren't many tourists, so I got to look at the models and the artifacts pretty much by myself. Arjay and I stayed away from each other through some unspoken rule. You kinda want to be alone with something that devastating, with the guilt of something that happened before you were born but you know it's still somehow your fault. It's embarrassing to share with other people. Those are some of my best moments in museums.

(Lights up more fully. SCHILLER *is looking at an exhibit. A rather scruffy looking* STUDENT *approaches* SCHILLER.)*

STUDENT: *Sprechen-zie Deutsche?*

SCHILLER: *Nein,* English, sorry. *(Steps away a bit)*

STUDENT: *(Following. Russian accent)* What do you think of this?

SCHILLER: I can't imagine anything worse.

STUDENT: Do you think it could happen again?

SCHILLER: Not exactly this way, but yes, I'm afraid it could.

STUDENT: Why is that?

SCHILLER: I'm sorry, I wanted to—

STUDENT: I don't mean to disturb you, but I'm curious. Why do you think it could happen again?

SCHILLER: People haven't changed. Not enough, anyway. That's why we should never forget.

STUDENT: So it is human nature?

SCHILLER: I guess.

STUDENT: Could it be something else?

SCHILLER: *(Trying to concentrate on the exhibit)* I suppose.

STUDENT: Could it be money?

SCHILLER: Money?

STUDENT: Economic exploitation.

SCHILLER: I think this was ethnic hatred, racism—

STUDENT: The Jews had the money. Hitler wanted it.

SCHILLER: It's more complicated than that—

STUDENT: Capitalism is complicated, but if you can see through it—

SCHILLER: Excuse me. *(Leaves)*

STUDENT: *(Calling after* SCHILLER*)* You're American, aren't you?

(Lights fade on the STUDENT *and come up on* ARJAY *and* ROGER.*)*

ROGER: I don't know why she'd want to see that.

ARJAY: Morbid curiosity?

ROGER: But...right now? It's strange to me.

ARJAY: But if she wants to—

ROGER: I want her to do whatever she wants to do—

SCHILLER: *(Entering)* What does she want to do?

ROGER: Where were you? Buying Nazi souvenirs in the gift shop?

SCHILLER: I got accosted by a Communist.

ARJAY: There are still Communists?

SCHILLER: It was like talking to someone from another time. A complete anachronism. What's she want to do?

ROGER: Your mother's been seeing ads for an exhibition—

ARJAY: You've seen them, on buses—

ROGER: *Corperwelten.* It means *Body Worlds.*

SCHILLER: She doesn't want to see *that*, does she?

ARJAY: Evidently.

SCHILLER: Does she know what it is?

(Lights up slowly on MILDRED *gazing at a* NUDE. *At first it seems like merely a sculpture, but as the lights rise, it is revealed to be an actual person in a strong pose, with one portion of the body opened up so that the muscles or organs are on view.)*

ROGER: I think so.

ARJAY: Is it really dead bodies?

SCHILLER: You remember—it came to L A again last year. This doctor talked a bunch of people into willing him their bodies, then he plastinated 'em and put 'em on display.

ROGER: Plastinated?

SCHILLER: It's some chemical process that infuses the bodies with enough plastic to completely prevent deterioration. He says it's educational, like medical students studying cadavers, but I think it's pure exploitation. He's even got a pregnant woman and her fetus.

ROGER: He got her permission?

SCHILLER: Only a German would think of something like that. At Natural History we've got a policy against the display of human remains. And Mom wants to see it?

ROGER: That's what she said.

ARJAY: I wouldn't mind. From an anatomical point of view.

SCHILLER: She's not going to like it.

ROGER: Are you going to tell her no?

(*Lights out on* ARJAY *and* SCHILLER *as* ROGER *joins* MILDRED, *who is looking at the* NUDE. ROGER *avoids looking at it.*)

ROGER: Mildred, I think I'll wait for you outside. I'm a little—you know how I am with blood—and this is much—

MILDRED: I won't be long.

ROGER: They're not even in cases. Right out where you could touch 'em if you wanted to—

MILDRED: You go. I understand.

ROGER: There must be fifty of them. I don't get why people would let someone do this to them, put them on display—it's funny, but the horse bothers me the most.

MILDRED: You should get some air.

ROGER: I will. But are you all right?

MILDRED: I'm fine.

ROGER: How can you even stand to look—?

MILDRED: They're talking to me, Roger.

ROGER: What?

MILDRED: Even dead, frozen like this, they have something to say.

ROGER: Bury me?

MILDRED: Oh, Roger, be serious.

ROGER: You be serious.

MILDRED: They talk. If you watch closely, they talk.

(ROGER *finally brings himself to look at the* NUDE. *He forces himself to scrutinize it. While he is staring,* MILDRED *leaves. After a moment, the* NUDE *moves.*)

NUDE: *(German accent)* You want to know what it's like, don't you?

ROGER: What…what's like?

NUDE: I hear you're going to Buchenwald.

ROGER: Did Mildred tell you that?

NUDE: I went there as a child. They make us.

ROGER: I don't want to go, but I feel it's my responsibility.

NUDE: As an American?

ROGER: As a human being.

NUDE: You are frightened.

ROGER: Some things you just have to do. You can't shrink.

NUDE: Mildred doesn't seem frightened.

ROGER: She's resigned.

NUDE: But still frightened, in secret. Hold her hand.

ROGER: I will.

NUDE: And she'll hold yours.

ROGER: What did you...die of?

NUDE: Cancer. Can't you see? That's why they opened me up. *(Points)*

ROGER: *(Peering)* Oh, that's awful. Did it hurt much?

NUDE: *Ja.* But they gave me opium at the end. Which was nice.

(ROGER just stares.)

NUDE: You want to touch, don't you?

ROGER: No!

NUDE: You want to touch.

(The NUDE reaches for ROGER, who faints. Lights up on MILDRED and ARJAY staring into the distance.)

MILDRED: Oh, ish. Are they—?

ARJAY: I think so.

MILDRED: —Americans?

ARJAY: They look like American *Lutherans.*

MILDRED: It's not nice to stereotype.

ARJAY: Look at them: pale, confused—

MILDRED: Fat.

ARJAY: I wasn't going to say that.

MILDRED: But it's true. Americans look fat out of context. Everyone in Europe is so trim.

ARJAY: Too much dairy.

MILDRED: Do we look like that?

ARJAY: We're dressed better. And we're not all huddled on a bus with others of our kind.

MILDRED: Oh, no—do you think—?

ARJAY: *(Quickly hands her a guidebook)* Here, pretend to read. *(Consults phone)*

MINNESOTAN: *(Appearing, wearing shorts and looking like a giant six year-old)* Hello! *Sprechen-zie Englisch?*

(They try not to notice, but MILDRED can't help a polite smile.)

MINNESOTAN: You must speak English. Your book is English.

MILDRED: Oh, hello.

ARJAY: Sorry, were you talking to us?

MINNESOTAN: Oh, great, you're Americans!

ARJAY: Um…yes.

MINNESOTAN: Where are you from?

ARJAY: Los Angeles.

MILDRED: Oklahoma.

MINNESOTAN: That's my group over there. We're on a pilgrimage, sorta, all the way from Mankato, Minnesota.

ARJAY: Ding, ding, ding!

MINNESOTAN: Excuse me?

MILDRED: Is it a Lutheran pilgrimage?

MINNESOTAN: You bet. We spent two days in Wittenborg, saw the Schlosskirke where Luther posted the 95 Theses, Melancthonhaus, Lutherhaus, of course, and now we're in Weimar—the heart, the soul of Germany—to see Goethehaus, Liszthaus, the Bauhaus, Schillerhaus—

ARJAY: Schillerhaus? What's that?

MINNESOTAN: Schiller was a playwright, nineteenth century, I think. *(Shows guidebook, the same as ARJAY's.)*

Been reading, but it all runs together in my head.
Uffda!

ARJAY: I didn't know that. About Schiller.

MINNESOTAN: Say, have you been keeping up with the
news?

MILDRED: I managed to find C N N two days ago for
about half an hour.

MINNESOTAN: So you don't know the latest?

ARJAY:	MILDRED:
We've only got one	What?
phone with terrible	
reception and battery life.	

MINNESOTAN: I'm trying to find out. Something about
the possibility of martial law in the U S.

MILDRED & ARJAY: Martial law!?

MILDRED: I knew it—he'll declare martial law so he can
hold onto the presidency.

MINNESOTAN: And I'm guessing the international
situation's worse, cause the Germans seem a little less
friendly every day. Have you noticed that?

MILDRED: Maybe a little.

MINNESOTAN: I feel so isolated traveling like this. I'm
not used to it. Every morning at home I sit down to the
newspaper and a cup of Tang tea. I don't know what's
going on and it kinda bugs me.

MILDRED: Last I heard it was worse, yes. New U N
resolutions, sanctions—

MINNESOTAN: We're sposed to fly out of Frankfurt in
two days. Hope we can get home.

ARJAY: Not really a good time to be traveling.

MINNESOTAN & MILDRED: But it's cheap!

(MINNESOTAN *laughs.* MILDRED *is embarrassed.*)

MINNESOTAN: You don't think anything really serious is going to happen, do you?

MILDRED: I'm sure not. It's all threats and posturing.

ARJAY: Saber-rattling. Mine's bigger than yours.

MINNESOTAN: Sure.

MILDRED: *(After a moment)* Well, have a wonderful trip back.

MINNESOTAN: Thanks. It's nice to see Americans— other than our group, I mean.

ARJAY: Especially if the Germans are being mean.

MINNESOTAN: You bet. We gotta stick together! *(Pause)* Well...*auf weidersehen.*

MILDRED:	ARJAY:
Good-bye.	Take care.

(MINNESOTAN *leaves, reluctantly.*)

ARJAY: *(After a moment)* Why didn't you say—?

MILDRED: I just didn't feel like it.

ARJAY: Schiller never told me—you never told me—

MILDRED: Told you what?

ARJAY: Is Schiller named for the playwright?

MILDRED: It was Roger's idea. At first he wanted Goethe, but imagine *that* on the playground.

ARJAY: What didn't you feel like saying?

MILDRED: It's amazing how just a few weeks away makes me not want to be an American. Oh, I don't mean that exactly, but I don't want to be associated with America right here, right now. Normally I would have said I was from Minnesota. But I just didn't feel like it. And I went to Mankato State!

ARJAY: I've seen you make that geography connection with strangers more than once.

MILDRED: My mother did it, too. She said if you ask enough questions, everybody's your cousin. Funny how right now I want to feel disconnected. Oh, that sounds awful.

ARJAY: No, it's okay. You feel free. Or at least freer.

MILDRED: Maybe that's it.

ARJAY: *(After a moment)* It wasn't me that persuaded you to come on this trip, was it?

(MILDRED *just smiles.)*

ARJAY: Was it finding out you were sick?

MILDRED: Schiller's always telling us our time is limited.

ARJAY: Schiller is almost always right.

MILDRED: They say when you travel you learn more about yourself than any place you visit.

ARJAY: For most people it's the last thing we want to know. *(Pause)* So—who are you?

MILDRED: I'm not finished yet. But I do know I'm not nearly as afraid as I used to be. *(After a moment)* Arjay, can you do us a favor?

ARJAY: I guess.

MILDRED: Roger and I are somewhat ambivalent about marriage—

ARJAY: I kinda got that.

MILDRED: Truth be told, we almost gave up on it ourselves a few years ago—

ARJAY: Schiller never told me—

MILDRED: Just seemed like a bad habit we were too lazy to break. Which must be true 'cause here we still are. But I don't regret that.

ARJAY: Now.

MILDRED: Now. *(After a moment)* Can you—not now, but someday—tell Schiller Roger and I almost split?

ARJAY: You mean you didn't—?

MILDRED: Sometimes it's hard to tell Schiller things.

(ARJAY just laughs.)

MILDRED: So you will? Someday?

ARJAY: Someday.

MILDRED: Roger and I are very happy you're marrying Schiller.

ARJAY: I know.

MILDRED: Of course, you do—

ARJAY: But that you can say so is even better.

MILDRED: *(After a moment)* Cause you should've seen what else Schiller's drug home! *(Bursts out laughing)*

ARJAY: *(Laughing)* You ruint it! You ruint it!

MILDRED: One spring break—oh, I'm glad Schiller's not here—one spring Schiller showed up on our doorstep with this perfectly nice—*person*—and we were all nervous and trying to be polite when suddenly while I was going on about—geography, I guess—doing my geographic connection thing—now that I know I have a *thing*—in the middle of me trying desperately to make this connection—Jamie—I think that was the name, Jamie—perfectly nice—suddenly pooted out, well, no, actually *blasted* out a nervous fart like you wouldn't believe. And I here I was, Mrs Gracious, Calm and Motherly, and I couldn't possibly even *acknowledge* this unfortunate explosion so I knew I had to keep talking but I had no idea what I'd been saying and just said the first words that came into my head—cat, dog, sigmoidoscopy, I don't remember what they were, but I know it didn't make any sense whatsoever! I just had to keep going or Schiller would be embarrassed and Roger and I would be embarrassed and Jamie the Poot Monster would shrivel and die and the whole mortified world would blow itself up!

ARJAY: Mildred, that was *me*. I pooted when I met you.

(MILDRED *gasps. Then she and* ARJAY *both burst out laughing, practically shrieking.* SCHILLER *and* ROGER *arrive at a trot.*)

SCHILLER: Mom, what's wrong?!

ROGER: Mildred, are you all right?

MILDRED: *(Laughing)* Nothing, yes, fine!

SCHILLER: Arjay, what's going on?

ARJAY: Nothing, just—remembrance of things passed.

(ARJAY *and* MILDRED *shriek again.*)

ROGER: When you've finished—

(ARJAY *and* MILDRED *try to stop but can't entirely.*)

ROGER: When you're over your seizures, I have some good news.

SCHILLER: We have a rendezvous in a graveyard.

ARJAY & MILDRED: What?

SCHILLER: Finally some genealogy for Mom.

ROGER: My mother's cousin's daughter is sending one of her children to meet us at— *(Looks at a scrap of paper)* —The Elephant, which I guess is a hotel—and then we'll all go to this cemetery to see the grave of Cousin Franz.

MILDRED: And who— *(Wiping away a tear)* —Sorry—
what is your mother's cousin's daughter's child's
name?

ROGER: *(Checks paper again)* Schlitzen.

ARJAY & MILDRED: What?

ROGER: Schlitzen!

(Lights come up isolating SCHLITZEN, *a tough customer,
possibly a skinhead.)*

MILDRED: Your mother's cousin's daughter's child is a
reindeer?

SCHLITZEN: I am Schlitzen.

*(Lighting changes so they are all in the same area. It is a bar
of an old hotel.)*

SCHLITZEN: *Wilkommen* to the Elephant.

ROGER: Schlitzen, I'm Roger. This is my wife,
Mildred—

MILDRED:	ARJAY:
Very nice to meet you.	I'm Arjay.

SCHILLER: And I'm Schiller.

SCHLITZEN: Funny name.

ARJAY: After the playwright!

*(*SCHILLER *looks at* ARJAY *in surprise.)*

SCHLITZEN: So you want to know my grandfather?

ROGER: Your whole family, really.

SCHLITZEN: Grossvater Franz came to this hotel for
drinking. It is most famous.

MILDRED: Famous for what?

SCHLITZEN: Was Hitler's favorite.

SCHILLER:	ROGER:	ARJAY
Really!	I'm not surprised.	Jesus!

SCHLITZEN: You know Grossvater was Nazi.

SCHILLER: ARJAY:
Everybody was.   No kidding!

ROGER: I'm not surprised.

SCHLITZEN: You are not shocked to have the Nazi relation?

ROGER: Was he a true believer?

(SCHLITZEN *looks confused.*)

ROGER: Or did he just go along for the ride?

SCHILLER: Dad, that's pretty colloquial.

SCHLITZEN: He joined for job, I think. In office, no killing. He did nothing. Too old to fight, so he made it safe through war.

ROGER: Did he have any hobbies?

SCHLITZEN: SCHILLER:
What are hobbies?   Colloquial.

ROGER: What did he do for fun?

SCHLITZEN: For fun? He did nothing. No, I am wrong. He enjoyed the theatre but hated the film. Before the war he went to Berlin to see Brecht. He enjoyed to watch.

ROGER: How funny! I teach theatre. I used to.

MILDRED: What do you do?

SCHLITZEN: For job?

MILDRED: Yes. Or are you in school?

SCHLITZEN: Dropped out. I live with Mutter.

ROGER: Have you been to Buchenwald?

SCHLITZEN: *Ja.* Not for long time, but does not change.

ROGER: Is it...well...I'm concerned I might not be able to take it. I passed out in that *Corperwelten* exhibition in Berlin.

SCHLITZEN: *(Shrugs)* You have seen the pictures.

ROGER: I don't think I want to go.

SCHILLER: MILDRED:
Dad!   Roger, you said yourself
                                  it's important.

SCHILLER: You can't come all the way to Germany and not go to a concentration camp. It's like visiting L A and not going to Disneyland.

SCHLITZEN: That is very funny. *(Gets up)* I give directions now.

MILDRED: You're not going with us?

ROGER: There's so much we want to ask you! The family, politics—!

SCHLITZEN: Politics?

SCHILLER: The international—you know—situation—kinda scary for us, traveling and all—

ROGER: The German position vis-à-vis our American perspective—

SCHLITZEN: There is no German position. There is the government, and there are real people. Government say "peace in our time", but we hear that before, don't we? German government so pure and holy because they have no choice. They cannot talk war. When everyone forget Hitler, maybe then. But the world forget the moon and sun before they forget Hitler.

ROGER: No, I don't think anyone will forget.

SCHLITZEN: I did not know Hitler. Yet I am one without the job. My hands— *(Shows them)* —Clean—no blood. The Jews are safe from me.

MILDRED: Are you feeling safer now?

SCHLITZEN: Safe? Now?

MILDRED: With the Soviets out of Germany, I mean.

SCHLITZEN: Safe from what? At the least Russians are predictable—we don't know what you'll do—

ROGER:	MILDRED:
Not us!	We're not our government either.

SCHLITZEN: I am sorry. I go now.

ROGER: Wait! Can you tell us any more about Franz, about anything…? Were you born before he—

SCHLITZEN: I knew him. Is nothing to tell. No, I am wrong once more. He died in theatre.

MILDRED: An accident?

(Lights out on everyone but SCHLITZEN*)*

SCHLITZEN: No. Sitting in seat. Watching.

(Lights out on SCHLITZEN *and up on* SCHILLER, ARJAY, MILDRED *and* ROGER *sitting on a bus)*

ROGER: Of all the narrative arts, theatre is superior.

ARJAY: How's that?

ROGER: It's the real thing. A book is just ink on pulp. Film is just light. Insubstantial. With theatre you get real actors right in front of you.

ARJAY: What about dance and opera?

ROGER: They're like theatre. *Gesamtkunstwerk* incorporating all the arts. Live.

SCHILLER: Exhibitions are narratives, too. With real objects, usually.

ROGER: But you don't have to follow a particular narrative. Nothing prevents you from jumping from display to display or even seeing the whole thing backward.

MILDRED: You can skip to the end of a book just as easily.

ROGER: Most people don't, Mildred. There's a fairly rigid expectation that books are read front to back. And not a word of a novel changes once it's published. Same for movies— *(Waving off* SCHILLER's *objection)* — Once they're released they don't change, arguments between the director and the studio notwithstanding. But theatre changes every night, from performance to performance, from production to production, with different actors, different designers, different direction, different audiences—it's so much more alive!

MILDRED: Please stop talking in circles on public transportation. I'm getting sick.

SCHILLER: When did you come up with all this?

ROGER: *(Shrugs)* I'm retired. I finally get to think.

MILDRED: You can imagine what it's like for me. I keep signing him up for volunteer work. *(Looking out the window)* Roger, are you sure this is the right bus? We're in the middle of the woods.

ROGER: It's supposed to be a country graveyard.

MILDRED: Could you ask the driver?

ROGER: I'm sure this is right.

SCHILLER: *(Starts to get up)* I can ask.

ROGER: You don't speak German.

SCHILLER: Most everybody speaks some English. And if you're too nervous—

ROGER: *(Stands)* I'm not nervous! *(Leaves)*

MILDRED: *(Watching him go)* Dad doesn't really speak German, you know. He can read it, I think. But when he can't be completely articulate, he gets shy.

ARJAY: After this cemetery, can we see the Bauhaus?

SCHILLER: Sure, it's close to the Hilton. *(On phone)* Dammit, I'm almost out of juice!

MILDRED: When are we going to Buchenwald?

SCHILLER: I think we've got some lobbying to do with Dad first.

ARJAY: He got so squeamish all of a sudden.

SCHILLER: I can't believe he fainted in Berlin. Is he all right?

MILDRED: An atrial fibrillation isn't trivial, Schiller.

ARJAY: Shhh!

ROGER: *(Returning)* I don't know what happened.

MILDRED: It's the wrong bus.

ROGER: No, it's the right bus. But it's the wrong schedule or something. The driver—it's so frustrating—I've forgotten so much German!—I think the driver said there are alternate schedules—

SCHILLER: Then we have to get off at the next stop.

MILDRED: How soon will that be?

ROGER: I don't know.

SCHILLER: Look, we're okay, I downloaded a map before my phone died, and I remember—

MILDRED: It died?

ARJAY: We're stopping.

SCHILLER: Good, okay, everybody get out.

(As they stand:)

ROGER: I'm sorry, Schiller.

SCHILLER: It's okay, Dad. Hurry, before the bus takes us all the way to Poland!

(Lighting change. SCHILLER, ARJAY, MILDRED, and ROGER are standing by the road in dappled sunlight.)

ARJAY: Why did we get off the bus?

SCHILLER: We were going the wrong way. A bus going back the way we came should be by any minute. Or—!

MILDRED: What?

SCHILLER: We could—no, never mind.

ROGER: Never mind what?

SCHILLER: I was gonna say we could walk.

ROGER: Back to Weimar?!

SCHILLER: No, of course not. But there's another place we could catch a bus sooner just down— *(Points)* — That road.

ROGER: How far?

MILDRED: Oh, Roger, you can't go hiking!

SCHILLER: It looks like two kilometers.

ROGER: What's that in miles?

SCHILLER: A little more than one.

ROGER: I can do that. If we don't rush.

MILDRED:	ARJAY:
Roger, no—	Don't they have Uber in Germany?

SCHILLER: My phone's dead! If a bus comes along we can wave it down.

ARJAY: And it will stop because…we look so pathetic?

SCHILLER: We're not pathetic. It'll be a nice walk in the shade, sunlight filtered through the trees.

MILDRED: It is pretty. Reminds me of Minnesota.

SCHILLER: And if it gets to be too much I can just run ahead and call a taxi to drive out from Weimar.

MILDRED:	ROGER:
Oh, no.	That's too expensive.

SCHILLER: Should we walk then?

(When they all look at him:)

ROGER: Yes, dammit, let's walk!

(They walk. Lighting change reveals a sign in Cyrillic. ROGER is looking sweaty and tired. They all look out over the audience.)

SCHILLER: Wow. Anybody read Cyrillic?

MILDRED: What's that? Is it Russian?

ROGER: Whatever it is, they didn't make it easy to find.

ARJAY: You could barely see it from the road.

MILDRED: It looks like a memorial.

ARJAY: It's Soviet design.

SCHILLER: Kinda scary.

(ARJAY gets close enough to the sign to read the panel underneath it.)

ROGER: What does the map say it is?

SCHILLER: This wasn't on the map.

ARJAY: This part's not in Russian.

ROGER: Is it in German? If it is, I'll come read it. If not, I'm not taking another step.

ARJAY: I think it's German.

ROGER: *(Going to the sign)* Let me see.

MILDRED: Look, there are names of countries.

SCHILLER: Where?

MILDRED: On those pedestals.

SCHILLER: Oh, yeah. *Auf Deutsche.*

MILDRED: Austria, Belgium, Czechoslovakia—

MILDRED & SCHILLER:	ROGER:
—Denmark, France,	*(Reading)*
Germany, Greece,	Denkmal…Todt…
Hungary, Italy, Latvia,	
Luxembourg, the	
Netherlands, Norway,	
Poland, Romania—	

ROGER: Schiller!

SCHILLER: What, Dad?

ROGER: I told you I didn't want to come here!

ARJAY: What is it?

MILDRED: *This* is Buchenwald?

SCHILLER: No, it's not. I've seen pictures. Buchenwald's nothing but old foundations—

ARJAY: Just like Manzanar in California—

SCHILLER: That's right—buildings built in the thirties and razed in the forties or fifties. It really does look exactly like Manzanar.

ARJAY: They're both concentration camps.

ROGER: America didn't have concentration camps.

MILDRED: If it's not Buchenwald, what is it?

ROGER: This is some kind of Soviet memorial to the people who died at Buchenwald, so the camp itself—

ARJAY: Must be close by.

MILDRED: Schiller, is that where you're taking us?

(SCHILLER, *for once, has nothing to say.*)

ARJAY: Guilty! Look at that Lutheran guilt!

ROGER: I am very irritated.

SCHILLER: I didn't plan it, I swear. But when I saw where the bus dropped us off, I thought we'd have a nice walk in the woods—

ROGER:	ARJAY:
I'm about to keel over!	And then—?

SCHILLER: We wouldn't have time to get nervous, we'd just be there all of a sudden. And if we'd taken the bus, we wouldn't have seen this whatever-it-is, since they seem to be trying to hide it.

MILDRED: *(Pointing)* What are those three depressions?

ROGER: Mass graves, according to that panel. The bodies are *right there.*

(They gaze silently at the graves for a moment. ROGER massages his chest.)

MILDRED: I will never, ever understand it.

ARJAY: Did the local people know this was happening in the woods just outside town?

SCHILLER: They say they didn't. But someone had to do business with the camp, make deliveries. There was even a zoo.

MILDRED: A zoo!

SCHILLER: For the entertainment of the guards' families.

ROGER: I have to sit down.

(ROGER sits on the ground. The others continue to stare at the site.)

SCHILLER: The bear pits still exist. You'll see when we get there.

MILDRED: It's not like an American memorial. So massive. Almost brutal.

ARJAY: Definitely Soviet design.

ROGER: Mildred…

MILDRED: *(Going to him)* Roger, what—?

ROGER: My chest is bothering me a little.

MILDRED: Your chest!

SCHILLER: Dad, what hurts?

ARJAY: Are you breathing okay?

SCHILLER: How about your arm?

ROGER: My arm, too.

(Sound of a bus approaching)

SCHILLER: Does it hurt a lot?

ROGER: Not a lot, but it's uncomfortable.

MILDRED: Schiller, there's a bus. Make it stop!

SCHILLER:	ROGER:
Oh, right!	No, it's not that bad….

SCHILLER:	ARJAY:
(Taking a few steps toward the bus)	*(Waving)*
Hey, there! Stop! Halt!	Help! Please!

(The bus does not stop.)

ARJAY: *(Chasing the bus for a bit)* Emergency! Stop! Please!

(The bus roars off into the distance.)

SCHILLER: I'm sorry.

ARJAY: I think we'll have to throw ourselves in front of the next one.

ROGER: It's okay. Maybe a car will come by.

MILDRED: It's not okay, Roger. You're having a heart attack. Schiller, you have to try harder.

SCHILLER: Mom—I will—

ROGER: I'm not having a heart attack. Just—out of breath from the walk.

MILDRED: We shouldn't have been walking.

SCHILLER: We'll stop the next one, Mom. Don't worry.
Or I can run the rest of the way to Buchenwald.
There'll be phones, taxis, buses, maybe even
emergency services—

MILDRED:	SCHILLER:
You can't leave. You're	It will take me less than
the only one who knows	fifteen minutes—
where we are.	

ARJAY: Here comes another bus!

(Sound of a bus approaching)

MILDRED: Schiller, please, jump in front of it if you
have to!

ROGER: Now, Schiller, don't get yourself killed!

ARJAY: *(Waving wildly)* Hey, stop! Help! Heart attack!
(To ROGER*)* How do you say "heart attack" in German?

ROGER: Hertz something.

(Both SCHILLER *and* ARJAY *wave.)*

ARJAY:	SCHILLER:
Hertz! Halt! Hertz!	Hello, please stop!

(Suddenly MILDRED *dashes past them out of sight and into
the path of the bus.)*

SCHILLER:	ARJAY:	ROGER:
Mother, no!	Look out!	Mildred, stop!

(Sound of the bus screeching to a halt)

SCHILLER: Oh, for God's sake, Mother! *(Dashes off)*

BUS DRIVER: *(Off) Verrüchtes Huhn, geh mir ans dem Weg!*
[Crazy lady, get out of the way!]

MILDRED:	SCHILLER:
(Off)	*(Off)*
You have to give us a ride!	He's having a heart attack.
My husband's sick.	Come, please!

BUS DRIVER: *(Off) Wissen Sie nicht was passiert ist? Drese Leute möchten nach Hause. Sie müssen auf der Stelle nach Hause! Und überhaupt—wes machs Du hie dranssen im Wald?* [Don't you know what's happening? These people want to get home! They need to get home right away! What are you doing out here in the woods, anyway?]

(Leading MILDRED *and* BUS DRIVER *to* ROGER:)

SCHILLER: *Sprechen-zie Englisch?*

BUS DRIVER: *Nein.*

SCHILLER: Dad, you'll have to translate.

BUS DRIVER: Americans?

ROGER:	SCHILLER:
Ja.	*Ja! Ja! Ich bin ein American.*

ROGER: *Mein hertz—*

BUS DRIVER: *Ihr habt sie fallen lassen!* [You dropped it!]

ROGER: *Was?*

BUS DRIVER: *Ihr habt die Bombe fallen lassen!* [You dropped the bomb!]

ROGER: I did not! *Nein! Nein!*

BUS DRIVER:	MILDRED:
Es ham im Radio—	What's he saying? Tell him
habt ihr's nicht gehört?	about your heart!
[It's on the radio!	
Haven't you heard?]	

ROGER: *Mein hertz, bitte—*

BUS DRIVER: *Eine Atomwaffe! Ihr arroganten Schweine! Eine stadt ist ausgelöschl! Millionen von Monschen. Die ganze Welt ist jetzt gegen Euch!* [A tactical nuclear device! You arrogant bastards. A city is gone! Millions of people. The whole world is against you now!]

SCHILLER:	ROGER:
(Accosting the BUS DRIVER*)*	Oh, my God. We didn't!
Take us to Weimar!	
Weimar! Hospital!	

BUS DRIVER:	ARJAY:
(Pushing SCHILLER	Hey, what are you—?
violently away)	
Rühr mich nicht an!	
Du bist ummöglich.	
[Don't touch me!	
You are despicable.]	

MILDRED: Schiller! *(Getting in the* BUS DRIVER's *face.)* My husband needs your help. Roger, how do you say "help"?

ROGER: *Helfen…helfen….*

MILDRED: *Helfen! Bitte!*

*(*ROGER *collapses.* MILDRED *and* SCHILLER *rush to him.)*

MILDRED:	SCHILLER:
Roger, no!	Dad, hang on!

BUS DRIVER: *Nun seid ihr allein! Ihr Idioten!* [You are on your own! Idiots!] *(Leaves)*

ARJAY: No, you can't leave us here! *(Follows* BUS DRIVER *off.)* That man might be dying! HELFEN! HELFEN, BITTE!

ROGER: I'm all right.

SCHILLER: You just collapsed!

ROGER: I can't believe it.

MILDRED:
Roger, what's going on?
Why wouldn't—it's
obvious we need help—
even if you can't
understand English—

ARJAY:
(Off)
Don't go! *Bitte!*

(Sound of the bus driving away)

SCHILLER:
Oh, no!

ARJAY:
You goddam Nazi!

ROGER: I can't believe we did it.

MILDRED: What did we do?

SCHILLER: We didn't do anything! We just wanted help.

ARJAY: *(Returning)* Roger, hang in there, I'll run to the camp. Okay? Schiller can stay and I'll run for help.

ROGER: It doesn't hurt so much right now. Maybe it was just gas. I had ice cream.

SCHILLER: What was all that about?

ROGER: Nothing.

SCHILLER: Nothing? I think I twisted my ankle!

ROGER: My German isn't perfect, you know—

MILDRED: But you understood something—

ROGER: Apparently— *(Fighting back tears)* —Oh, it can't be true. I'm not even going to tell you.

SCHILLER:
What?

MILDRED:
Please, Roger.

ROGER: I must have heard it wrong.

SCHILLER: What did you hear?

ROGER: It sounded like America just detonated a tactical nuclear weapon.

ARJAY:
Jesus!

MILDRED:
Oh, my heavens.

ROGER: The bus driver heard it on the radio.

SCHILLER: Against civilians?

ROGER: A city. I didn't hear which one, but—

MILDRED: We can guess.

(They are all silent for a moment, stunned.)

SCHILLER: Goddammit, Dad!

MILDRED: Our stupid, stupid president!

ARJAY: We elected him.

MILDRED & ROGER: We did not!

SCHILLER: I'm sure you heard it wrong.

ROGER: That's what I said.

MILDRED: We should have been paying more attention.

ARJAY: We wouldn't just—

SCHILLER: You're right. It doesn't make sense—a pre-emptive strike—

MILDRED: This isn't the first time we've dropped the Bomb.

ROGER: Mildred, I'm sure I was mistaken. Or the bus driver was confused—

ARJAY: We wouldn't *do* that!

MILDRED: We've done it twice before.

ROGER: Those were very different.

SCHILLER: Very!

MILDRED: Strike three.

ARJAY: True or not, we'll have to go back right away.

MILDRED: I don't want to go back.

ROGER: The only other place we speak the language is England, and they don't believe in washcloths. *(Starts to get up)*

SCHILLER: No, Dad, don't! Sit!

ROGER: I'm feeling better.

ROGER:	SCHILLER:
It hardly hurts at all now.	Just sit! Please! The best thing you can do is sit.

MILDRED: But rest for a bit anyway. It still hurts some, doesn't it?

ROGER: A little. But I can walk, I think.

SCHILLER: No!

ROGER: Schiller, stop telling me what to do! I know what I can do!

SCHILLER: You can die of a coronary is what you could do!

ROGER: I can't just sit. Let's go to Buchenwald. We can take it slow and I'll be fine. Then a taxi to Weimar, to the hospital, and I can get this checked out.

MILDRED: If they'll admit an American.

SCHILLER: Mom, it's not true, okay?

ROGER:	ARJAY:
I'll be fine.	No, I'm sure it's not.

MILDRED: Schiller, sometimes the worst thing is absolutely true. The worst thing! And you just have to accept it.

ROGER: Not in this case.

ARJAY: No.

SCHILLER: Of course not.

MILDRED: Let's not argue. *(Smiles)*

SCHILLER: *(After a moment, motioning* ARJAY *aside)* Arjay.

*(*SCHILLER *and* ARJAY *step aside as* MILDRED *silently attends to* ROGER, *wiping at his face with a tissue from her purse.)*

SCHILLER: *(Quietly to* ARJAY) He's really stubborn—

ARJAY: He can't walk that far—

SCHILLER: Who knows—he might. But arguing with him's only going to make it worse. Maybe on the way we can flag down a passing car—

ARJAY: Do you think your dad's going a little—you know—?

SCHILLER: No, but his German sucks.

ARJAY: Oh, look—

(ARJAY *and* SCHILLER *watch silently as* MILDRED *helps* ROGER *to his feet.)*

ARJAY: Us in thirty years, baby.

ROGER: *(Disengaging himself from* MILDRED) I can walk, Mildred, really.

MILDRED: Roger, are you sure?

ROGER: Schiller, let's march!

SCHILLER: We shouldn't if you have any pain at all.

ROGER: Then I don't.

SCHILLER: None?

ROGER: That's correct.

SCHILLER: Okay.

(They start to walk.)

SCHILLER: But very, very slowly.

ARJAY: You're the one who's always rushing.

MILDRED: Please don't argue. Please.

ROGER: We'll get there soon enough, Schiller. We're practically there already.

(They walk off as the lights fade.)

END OF PLAY

Made in the USA
Monee, IL
09 January 2023

24935213R00046